T0128258

DIMENSIONS OF THE MIND BODY SOUL SPIRIT AND UNIVERSE

BRUCE CONNOLLY

authorHOUSE®

AuthorHouse™
1663 Liberty Drive
Bloomington, IN 47403
www.authorhouse.com
Phone: 833-262-8899

Published by AuthorHouse 01/30/2023

ISBN: 978-1-7283-7868-8 (sc)
ISBN: 978-1-7283-7866-4 (hc)
ISBN: 978-1-7283-7867-1 (e)

Library of Congress Control Number: 2023901613

Print information available on the last page.

Dedicated to my son Pat. Please be enlightened!

CONTENTS

CHAPTER 1

BEGINNING

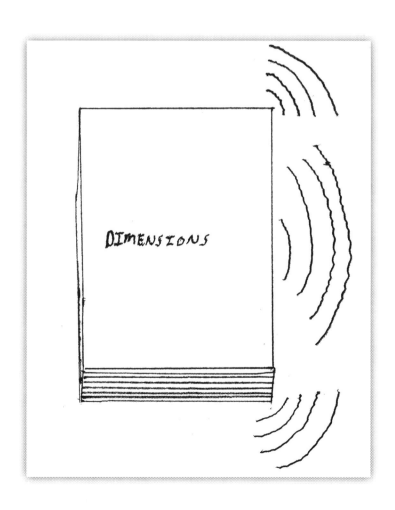

The science of the dimensions of the mind, body, soul, and spirit and how interaction occurs among these dimensions and our universe exist and which of these bonds exist at what time. Have we identified even a fraction of them?

What is dimension? It is a measurable extent of some kind—in this case, the mind, body, soul, and spirit and our universe. We will explore how these dimensions interact within each other.

The person's mind, body, soul, spirit, and universe continually develop as one ages, moving through time. There are pathways among these dimensions. As some pathways grow and become clear and open up, others may get fuzzy and less clear or disappear.

Essentially, the mind, body, soul, spirit, and universe begin for a person at birth, and for most people, they gravitate at end of living with their mind, heart's essence, soul, spirit, and aura of a person to the part of the universe or beyond known as heaven through a path. Heaven is defined in more detail in each person's religion. This is known as how the light of the living person carries on eternally. However, each religion may describe this transfer a bit differently. None is necessarily incorrect; they have developed their own interpretations.

The mind gives a person the ability to think and feel and memory to be aware of their world, their life experiences, and how they fit into the universe. This universe includes the method they live their lives for—a good and holy life to reach the good and holy part of the universe with their soul and spirit through their religious ways of living. For all religions in all likelihood, the good and holy way of living would reach this eternal goal for a person: the heavens.

The Tower of Babel in the Bible may indeed have been a repository of languages and religions with similar meanings for the passion of the Lord and Christ throughout the earth and other planets throughout the universe—for all of the kingdoms of the Lord when written. Similar towers may exist on other planets or kingdoms of the Lord throughout our universe. This meaning (repository to an extent) may have been lost through time on certain planets; however, the religions and languages carry on.

It stands to reason if reparation of a person's soul, spirit, heart's essence, and aura does not happen in the person's life through living a complete, good, holy life described in their religion, then there may be a temporary holding spot for this reparation to occur before entrance into the Lord's and Jesus's eternal kingdom of heaven can occur. Although some religions call this temporary reparation area differently, it is synonymous with purgatory. Not an area of punishment in all probability but an area of reparation.

Very few people who do not lead good, holy lives but choose dark evil, like a Devil or a person acting as the hand of the Devil, would in all likelihood end up in the eternal place known as hell. These are the terrorists of humanity. There would be no such area in hell as Valhalla or hell being Valhalla itself. All were dark, evil terrorists of humanity, the offenders of humanity. Hell in all probability is not a kingdom of the Lord but an area to hold the lost souls to protect heaven.

The people who defend the Lord's flock from the Devils and Devil's hand or Devil's acting hand would in all probability end up in the eternal resting place of heaven. Allowed into a special area of heaven known as Valhalla, an area for guardians of people to gather. Not necessarily an area to celebrate but to gather.

CHAPTER 2

PYRAMID

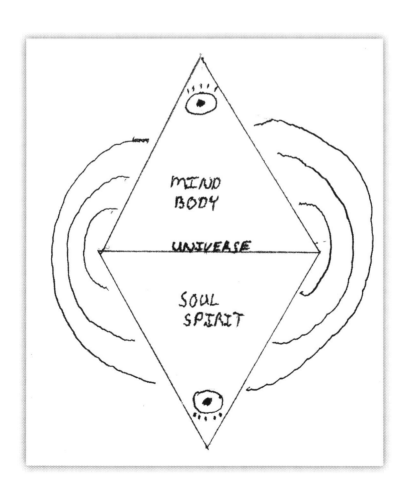

The three sides of a pyramid for a healthy person are the mind, body, and soul/spirit and how these evolve in the person's world and universe. What can be done to set these in a balanced course, and what happens in our universe that can set these off-balance? If we do get off-balance within us or by the world or universe around us, how can we be mindful of these balance inhibitors and get back on balance and in harmony?

The dimension of the mind as the function of the brain sends and receives chemical and electrical signals throughout the body. Different signals control different processes, and your brain processes each. This is genetically predisposed but can change by outside factors throughout a person's life. For example, if you were born without a limb, you may have to develop the path or wiring for the prosthetic limb. This is also true for how one path to a sense compensates for another that is lost or diminished. Also a person develops their processes and functions as they age and may lose some processes and functions as they age.

You process touch, sight, sound, smell, and emotion of the world we are immersed in. We can bring these senses into our minds and process them and express them as the person we have developed into. As these processes develop and the mind learns and develops, the memory helps evolve a person into the personality we become.

A healthy body allows the mind a better chance to operate in a healthy mode as well. A regimen of exercise helps keep the body fit and the senses keen. Getting regular professional checkups is a must for our bodies' dimensions of touch, sight, sound, smell, and emotional senses to stay in balance and harmony with our minds' and universe's dimensions.

Most people operate at peak if their soul/spirit dimension is also in harmony and balance with their minds' and bodies' dimensions. If a person is at peace with their faith, their life values, and morals through their religion, this resonates to other family members and creates a positive living atmosphere. This is a lifelong passion to oneself, to one's family, to the Lord's passion, and to Jesus's passion, which is priceless. This passion is expressed with oneself, family, and parishioners' prayers with the Lord and Jesus. This resonates to family values that are expressed to oneself in habits and how one interacts with family members and society.

If a person has all of these working in good accord, they can stay in relatively good balance and harmony. This would also lead the person to fit in a good balance and harmony with their family and universe.

If a country can also make this a goal for the people, the country also would be in good balance and harmony with the universe.

CHAPTER 3

BALANCE

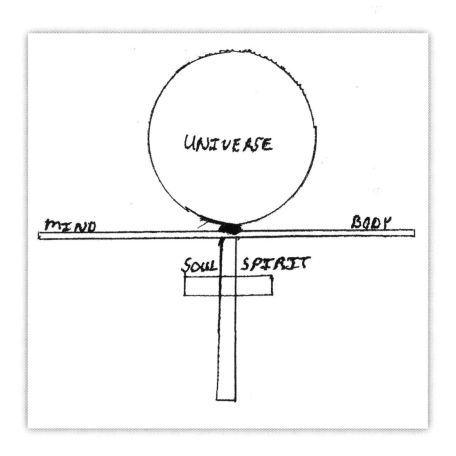

A person functions just fine under normal circumstances and even sometimes functions better with a bit of pressure. Too much pressure can be detrimental to performance and over a long period of time even more detrimental. That is why breaks and vacations are much required. Family, friend, and leisure time are so beneficial. Time to oneself may be priceless. Too much time to oneself is detrimental.

Education, training, and guidance absolutely help a person with expressing themselves successfully in our world today. Also common sense and self-help come into play.

Seeking help from family, religious personnel, educational personnel, and medical professionals helps guide a person greatly in reaching their life ambitions.

The educational personnel who are guidance counselors are great resources to help set a healthy path and should be sought at all ages as people's interests and challenges change continually through their life. Even at a young age, take an interest test to help guide you and take them periodically through life as interests develop and change. Guidance counselors should be sought for the very young and periodically—and as needed throughout a person's life.

By keeping mindful and using meditating strategies to help keep a person in harmony and balance, a person attains a healthy life. A daily logbook of activities, of to-dos, and of food consumption helps a person stay in balance. Also listing goals that you want to strive for helps a person keep level.

CHAPTER 4

STRESS

Throughout a person's life, we all run into some very stressful challenges. In a mental health crisis for yourself or another, first responders (police) can help you with a 911 call (in the USA), to get you help to the correct guidance personnel. Absolutely *call!* Do not delay.

What is a mental health crisis? It is when people are in danger of bringing harm to themselves or others or simply have lost their reasoning ability. This may be easier to recognize in other people but difficult to identify in oneself. If you do recognize this difference in yourself, *just get help immediately!* If others recognize this difference in you or someone, *just get help immediately!*

What are these stressors? Events in people's lives of all ages, pretty much from birth to the end of life. These could be caused by changes in natural events. Personal health changes in you or others who come in contact with you. Change events by our physical environmental challenges. Relationship events between people and groups of people can be stressful throughout a person's life.

A big stress is nature's cataclysmic events. The damage they create through hurricanes, tornados, winds, hail, floods, rain, snow, sleet, ice, etc. can be devastating in a person's life.

Health changes in you or loved ones can definitely put stress in your life, your loved ones' lives, and in the lives of all the people around you. Both physical and mental health changes can be very challenging. Loss of a loved one is a real hardship.

Another big stress entails changes in our physical environments. Road construction or overcrowding on the road system tax a person's patience and can be hard to deal with. There are many others such as overcrowding in various situations. It can be a lost feeling.

Another big stress is our relationship between people and even ourselves. Performance expectations are with us through a good share of our lives. These can be in almost all facets of our lives, jobs, education, sports, games, etc. This stress can degrade a person's performance and enhance a person's performance. This is where the proper amount of rest comes into play.

CHAPTER 5

TERRORISM

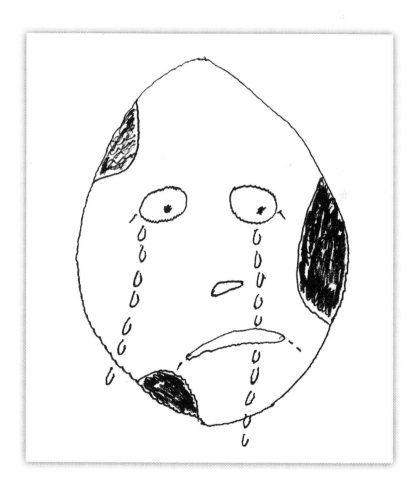

The biggest stress known to humans that is controllable by at least part of the population is the act of war, a direct offense of terrorism. This is a deplorable act of humans; differences should always be determined peacefully. The right side of war is the defense side. Rather than enter a wrong side of the offensive act of terrorism, we should always try to bring a peaceful resolution to the problem or conflict at hand. Before a terroristic war begins, if ambassadors can bring the differences to a peaceful resolution, of course, this is always best for humanity's sake; it keeps balance and harmony in place. Also the amasadorism should not turn into an offense of terrorism itself.

An extremely horrible form of terrorism would be people playing a game of terrorism that victimizes people criminally. A deplorable act of humankind. A sickness, like a bully, that is certainly not an acceptable form of human behavior. This would also be considered an act of offensive terroristic war.

An act of war of terrorism of any kind and even for sovereignty is also unacceptable. At this point of humanity, these issues should be resolved diplomatically. This physical loss of life and limb and destruction of homeland is a horrendous act of humanity.

A physical terroristic war by a kingdom or government may use a variety of weaponry or tools of warfare, such as spacecraft, satellites, jets, planes, ships, tanks, cannons, bullets, drones, and missiles armed with projectiles or wave objects to destroy or maim people and structures.

Physical terroristic wars as well as mental terroristic wars are unwelcome and devastating to individual people and entire societies. Physical harm and emotional harm beyond belief can be done to each person and the society within the war's boundaries. Constant anxiety and fear exist. Stress of the person, family, community, and society has adverse effects on all that is constantly present. Excessive alcohol and drug use—legal or illegal—can skyrocket. Even mass shootings can transpire.

They can be launched through computer-aided devices.

One mental war of terrorism can be done telepathically to a person, family, community, and society where the adverse effects can be horrendous and cause mental health problems beyond belief. This type of terrorism can cause bipolar disorder, schizophrenia, dementia, Alzheimer's disease, and other mental health maladies that can outright lead to a person's end of life. These terroristic attacks can mislead a person into harmful and dangerous behavior for themselves and others. Not just minor mishaps through mind and memory disruption. They can lead to suicides and outright attacks on others, including mass shootings. They can cause a person's fatigue and cause personal and transportation accidents—many fatal. They can cause fear and anxiety and lead to poor decision-making of the person they are attacking and society they are attacking. These can be specific in nature and widespread in nature. They can cause emotional problems in personal relationships and financial instability.

They can be launched through computer-aided devices.

Another kind of terroristic war can be done telekinetically to a person and the electronics in our society and to our physical surroundings through kinetic waves. These attacks can also have extreme physical and mental maladies on a person, family, community, and society. They can also create physical damage to our environment that surrounds us. The electronics can be our TVs, DVDs, computers, cell phones, appliances, vehicles, planes, trains, automobiles, etc. Also the attack could be the people themselves, itchiness, the digestive system, a person's movements being somewhat altered, etc. Not limited to minor irritations, they can cause mishaps and maladies, such as a person falling, car accidents, train accidents, and plane accidents. These can be specific in nature and widespread in nature. They can even cause misdirection in our societies to pets we hold so dearly.

They can be launched through computer-aided devices.

Further terroristic attacks are known as hacking. This may be for financial gain of the hacker via computers and phones to raid bank accounts and may to cause irreparable damage to the devices and their software.

Another kind of tool that may be used terroristically is subliminal messages through our communications network. This network is large and not inclusive to this list: TVs, radios, satellites, computers, cell phones, etc. These can be used to misdirect a person or group of people. They can express political views, personal care of people, and even how much a person eats. This makes people weaker rather than stronger—the same as the society under attack.

They also can be launched through computer-aided devices.

A war of terror of all this can lead to mental slavery or Nazism in a country and surrounding countries. This comes at horrible costs to the people and the countries, including losing their freedoms such as speech. They would lose their rights as human beings, and they would lose their God-given rights and entitlement as human beings. They would be ruled by fear. They could hold job positions over a person as a financial means to control them at their beck and call. They could also frame people into various sex stings to control them into their schemes. With telepathic and telekinetic terrorist attacks, they could disable a person or part of a society to function sexually. This could become extreme Nazism whereby terrorists are creating a society of terrorists as slaves.

This could actually result in a terroristic civil war within a government. Part of the government could be the offending terrorists.

This could also be a criminal syndicate that operates legally in a government but has corrupted the government in the operation of its country. These would be considered criminals all the same.

A war could be inflicted through a virus by a Devil on an entire world such as COVID. This war could inflict a horrible loss of life and well-being. The whole world would have to unite to battle this war of terrorism.

These terrorists would be considered a country's and kingdom's criminals. They are using tools of humanity the wrong way criminally in an offensive nature rather than a defensive nature so they can destroy people and possibly their environments as offenders rather than save and protect people and their environments as defenders.

Societies' terrorists: Within a kingdom and government, criminals who are not part of the government itself victimize people intentionally for their personal gain and other personal reasons. These include thieves, vandals, extortionists, illegal drug distributors, murderers, and many others not listed here. This may also include criminal syndicates that operate illegally for personal gain. All kingdoms and governments have justice systems to bring these offenders to justice.

CHAPTER 6

PROPHECY

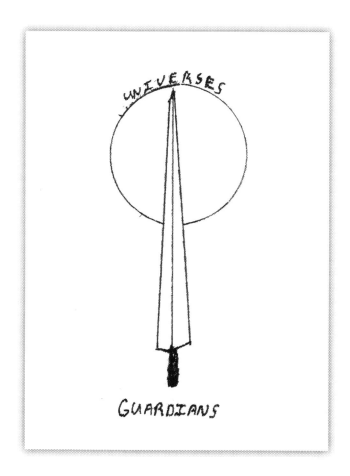

In the Dead Sea Scrolls, a prophecy was written toward the beginning of time that the Lord would answer these terrorists of humanity considered the Devils and Devil's hands—the dark evil of humanity that destroys humanity horribly and murderously and answers with a force of reckoning with the Beast, Manowar, Archangels of Light, and an alliance of the good and holy people to defeat these evil forces to save humans from a life of hell for the preponderance of humanity for all generations to come.

This will free all from the preponderance of terror and free all to choose the Passion of the Lord and Passion of Jesus to celebrate the passion of oneself.

I believe this time has come!

Virtual peace is close to being at hand. As close as it can be from terror from governing powers of control for all kingdoms of the Lord.

The Beast of the Lord is part of the Holy Spirit that is the church of the Lord that is returning God-given rights and entitlements to each person to be good and holy and a much more balanced and harmonious person and family.

The Manowar is part person and part machine that brings powers of the universe to defeat the Devils and the Devil's hands—the dark evil of the universe. The Beast is part of this defense. It brings the holy powers to remove the Devil's powers and to protect the Lord's flocks for the good and holy to remain victorious. The Lord God Almighty, Manowar, Beast, Archangels of Light in the universe, and an alliance of people beyond belief bring ultimate victory to the Lord God Almighty and his flocks in his kingdoms throughout the universe for the Passion of the Lord and the Passion of Jesus and all that is good and holy to be available to all human beings. This would open up the gate of kingdom of the Lord of heaven to the preponderance of human beings now and for all generations to come.

The Manowar and Beast are also a Lord that rides with the Lord God Almighty in defending his flocks and kingdoms.

To defend the human rights and entitlements of each person or family is not criminal. The right to correct the wrong of humanity certainly is not criminal. Having the terrorists who are criminal ruin the kingdoms of the Lord's flock brought to justice for their criminal actions is 100 percent required for the Lord's kingdoms and flocks to exist perpetually and out of the preponderance of a living hell environment.

To establish this justice environment, a criminal system must be installed over all kingdoms of the Lord in the living. This way, human beings who are flagged as criminal offenders would not be able to have power and control over other human beings. This would bring freedom from the preponderance of terrorism to all kingdoms of the Lord. This would include the return of freedom to the Lord's flocks and freedom of speech that was terroristically taken away. More of a checks and balance system to society from the very top.

This wrong of humanity of having the dark evil in power and control over the Lord's flocks and kingdoms will now be corrected for eternity! The Lord's flocks and kingdoms will now control their own destiny the right way!

CHAPTER 7

REPAIRS

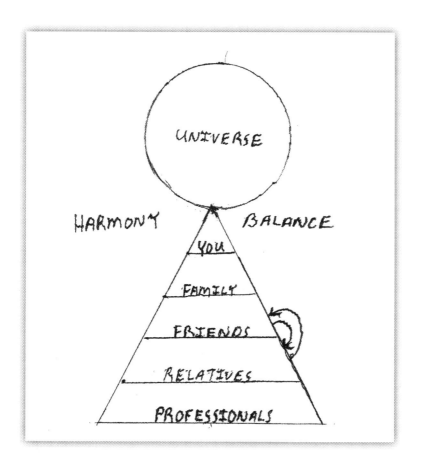

Reparation from these wars of terrorism must be done with great care and insight with the help of trained professionals. Some of the wars of terrorism are more hidden behind deceit and self-awareness to what's been going on with you and your family; once revealed, the truth will help immediately with reparation. Even if the wars have not virtually ended, it is time to start the reparation process with yourself, family, community, and your environment.

Our defense teams, military, medical teams, and educational teams in all societies that know right from wrong can help with repairing people and society. They will defend the people and the people the fit way from the offenders of humanity.

Mental reparation for you and your family can be aided with mental health counselors, psychologists, psychotherapists, and similar professionals. Education of all basic classes should be completed from math, science, health, sex education, history, language arts, music, arts, etc. in a fulfilling K through 12 program. Continued education is most likely required for career fulfillment in a vocational program or two- or four-year college course of choice or higher. Added classes may be needed to fulfill a new selection in a career path or enhance an existing career.

Body reparation for yourself and your family can be aided with trained medical doctors, nurses, therapists, and other medical personnel. Also personal trainers at gyms can aid greatly in helping a person recover. You can also aid this on your own by following a good fitness regimen.

Spirit/soul reparation for you and your family can be aided with trained religious personnel. Attending ceremonies and meetings where education transpires and is interactional, including music, can be an enlightening experience for you and your family. Symbolism is very important for many with art, signs, music, and food that heighten a person's senses of touch, smell, hearing, and sight to a higher self and a higher being with the Lord and Jesus. The clothing that people wear is also important in this symbolism of religious ceremonies. The clothing may indicate the respect and honor that transpire to each other and the Lord and Jesus. Jewelry and wares may be important as well as the worshipping structure itself.

By repairing these dimensions of a person who has been in a war of terrorism, the person and family can return to a more balanced and more harmonious state of being and belonging along with family members in this endeavor.

As the families repair in the society, the society becomes more balanced and harmonious.

The society can repair physical structures and infrastructure. Various discriminations—religious, racial, gender, ethnic, law and justice, mental capability, physical capability, age, and others—must be repaired for a more balanced and harmonious society. Right side and left side of politics may possibly lean in to help in this endeavor. We must put more guidance into place for all ages and more direction for help with identifying drug and alcohol problems in a society that has been in a terroristic war to recover successfully.

Acceptance of cultural differences, religious differences, gender differences, mental and physical differences, and law and justice differences must make great advances in a society for reparation from some of these wars of terrorism to heal properly. Education with training at all levels is a must for reparation to be successful.

Any act of war of offensive terrorism is considered an offense of a person, family, community, and an entire society that may include property damage and should never be tolerated. These offensive acts of terrorism that attack a person's God-given human rights and entitlements as a person are totally unacceptable.

If needed, the proper authorities should be called to help you protect your human rights!

This wrong needs to be corrected and righted!

The Lord God Almighty, Jesus, and the Holy Spirit would lead the way in these reparations! The Beast is part of the Holy Spirits themselves! The Manowar would also aid in this reparation endeavor with the power of the universe!

Truth!
Justice!
Freedom!
Liberty!
Unity!
Peace!

GOALS

Printed in the United States
by Baker & Taylor Publisher Services